ABOUT THE AUTHOR

Nadia Iris (Mitsiaris) has written poetry all her life and has been inspired by great thinkers, wise sages and unconventional writers along her journey. She now passes that gift onto future creators as a teacher and mentor to young adults. There is a common thread that runs within each of her poems: a frequency of love, truth and oneness. She hopes that this book will awaken the shine in all of us.

Nadia Iris

SHINE

Poems for the Awakened One

AUSTIN MACAULEY PUBLISHERS™

LONDON • CAMBRIDGE • NEW YORK • SHARJAH

A CIP catalogue record for this title is available from the British Library.

ISBN 9781528994736 (Paperback)
ISBN 9781528994743 (ePub e-Book)
ISBN 9781398442474 (Audiobook)

www.austinmacauley.com

First Published 2022
Austin Macauley Publishers Ltd
1 Canada Square
Canary Wharf
London
E14 5AA

For Teddy

And for those who are ready to awaken the light within

ACKNOWLEDGEMENTS

Teodor Chapanov, for inspiring me to share my light

Christina Chiminello,
for co-creating ideas for the illustrations

Luigia Milani-Van Zyl,
for guiding me towards a career in teaching

Viviana, Stefano and Tania,
for the unconditional love and support

Langden Batt, for bringing balance to the Libra within me

All those who believed in my message and donated towards the
publication of this book

My family and friends who believed in, encouraged and
supported my writing

Austin Macauley for believing in my message and allowing me
the opportunity to share my stories with the world

POEMS

STAR SIGNS

The concept of the star signs
Has been debated throughout time
So why not learn about them
Through a rhythm and a rhyme?

When we're looking at the night sky
We're not seeing just some dots
The stars can give us knowledge
And believe me there is lots!

When each of us is born to Earth
We have a birthing chart
And when you finally look at yours
You'll see some wondrous art

A birth chart is quite simply
The way the stars that night were placed
Exactly in the moment
In your body you embraced

It's how the stars all looked
Like a still picture in the sky
The moment that you entered Earth
And took your greatest cry

Now there's a misconception
In the wording we design
Your star sign is more properly
Called your very own "Sun Sign"

The way the planets move around
Passing each star sign
Makes the magic number 12
Not 3 or 6 or 9

For now let's start to understand
The signs, as there are many
There's no real order (kind of)
So we can start with any

The "general way" to follow
Says that we should start with Aries
Represented by a ram
Their approach to people varies

An Aries makes a statement
In your heart they will imprint
They're bold and optimistic
And are strong and confident

Being with an Aries
Means you should expect some fire
They're honest about who they are
And will call out a liar

Like everything in life
There is a good and negative
The weakness of an Aries
Is they can be aggressive

If someone wastes their talents
To an Aries they're repulsive
An Aries person can be moody
And sometimes quite impulsive

But overall you can expect
An Aries to bring fun
If you want a real party
This sign is the one

Moving through the sky
The way the stars lay out before us
We come across the steady bull
The star sign we call Taurus

A Taurus you can count on
This is undeniable
A Taurus is someone you know
Will be reliable

With never-ending patience
A Taurus one is still
They're who you need if
What you need is to be practical

On the other side of these good traits
Some bad ones are embedded
Like the tendency to often be
Quite stubborn and hard-headed

Their certainty in things they love
Makes them quite impressive
But when it comes to loved ones
A Taurus can be quite possessive

So to conclude the Taurus traits
You know what to expect
If you want a loyal partner
A Taurus is one to select

As the planets move around us
Through the stars and through the sky
The next star sign we meet
Is gentle Gemini

A Gemini is curious
Represented by the twins
Exchanging great ideas
Is where a Gemini begins

They love to have new knowledge
And are often quite progressive
The two sides of their beings
Are both certainly expressive

A Gemini won't hesitate
To speak of anything
It matters most to them
To try to experience everything

The trouble with a Gemini
Is they can be inconsistent
When making a decision
They can also be resistant

Their open-minded nature
Makes them really good at art
But they can also be quite nervous
To even make a start

If you're looking for the quality
Of affection in someone
And want someone who loves to talk
Then Gemini's the one

The next star sign we land on
Is a crab found in the sea
Our Cancer friends have mastered
The 'caring' quality

They're highly sympathetic
And always use their intuition
They connect to others deeply
With intelligent emotion

Sometimes a Cancerian
May become a tad suspicious
And if you hurt their loved ones
What they'll show you can be vicious

They like their friend group smaller
And stay away from strangers
They never share what's personal
Because there may be dangers

But if you're ever needing help
Or just want someone there
A Cancer should be chosen
Since all they do is care

There are infinite constellations
And one of them's Orion
Now as we move past Cancer
We approach Leo the Lion

You'll know you've met a Leo
Just by how they emanate
A vibrant energy
That always keeps them up-to-date

A Leo is a feisty one
Think how a Lion is
They're like a sweet champagne
With all the bubbles and the fizz

Creative at their core
They also work on being generous
You'll capture their attention
Just as long as you are humorous

The bad side of a Leo
Is they may have a big head
Opposed to being humble
They can be arrogant instead

They can also be quite lazy
And don't like a lot of change
And when talking of opinions
You'll find that they have a range

But the Lion is the King
And Leos deserve to have respect
'Cause in being with a Leo
A strong love you can expect

We're slowly moving forwards
As around the sky we spin
Our next star sign we meet
Is stunning Virgo – the Virgin

The Lady of the skies
Virgo is presented as a female
With an extremely loyal heart
They pay close attention to all detail

They are extremely tender
And like things to be planned out
They prefer to have a roadmap
So there's never room for doubt

Because of their deep kindness
Virgos like to be quite careful
They know that life's a mystery
And this can make them fearful

But there isn't any other sign
Who cares for the human race
As much as trusted Virgos
And so their fears they will face

So if you're looking for a partner
Or a husband or a wife
And want things to be perfect
You need a Virgo in your life

To plan a perfect party
A Virgo never fails
Now let's move on to meet the sign
Presented as the scales

A Libra may seem up and down
And can be quite erratic
But you will find they pride on being
Extremely diplomatic

You can count upon a Libra
To have a radiating charm
They're the ones you want
For some eye-candy on the arm

A Libra likes to move through life
With elegance and grace
You'll need a Libra with you
If you're fighting a court case

They love to have things balanced
And find justice in all wrongs
Smack bang in the middle
Is where this sign belongs

The negative of wanting
Everything to be so fair
Is that a Libra person
Is never here nor there

When making a decision
A Libra needs a little nudge
The negative about this sign
Is they can hold a grudge

They like to have self-pity
And will often blame a nation
They may insist on fairness
But dislike confrontation

A Libra wants world peace
And harmony for everyone
If you're looking for a balance
Then a Libra is the one

So now let us continue
Off to the stars we go
Next we see up in the sky
Our friends in Scorpio

The strength in Scorpio means sometimes
That they can be quite forceful
But when something must be done
They are abundantly resourceful

The scorpions have conviction
They'll always have their say
Their determination forces others
To move out of their way

Because they are so sure of things
They easily compel us
But something bad about this sign
Is that they can be jealous

They also can keep secrets
For a hundred years inside
They'll never share a story
If they have something to hide

So if you need a strong person
Or something to be done
Or even a great leader
Then a Scorpio's the one

Now who do we see next
Along the journey on our course?
It looks like Sagittarius
Half man and half a horse

Presented as an archer
With an arrow shooting high
They dislike making rules
And really struggle to comply

They're always looking forward
And are filled with energy
A Sag is often curious
About philosophy

The negative about this sign
Is that they cannot wait
Impatience about things they want
Is a dominating trait

Not getting what they want
Will put them in a sour mood
And they'll give their opinions
Even if they're sometimes rude

But if you want a leader
Who knows exactly where to go
And if you're lost and need a path
A Sag will surely know

Star sign number eleven
On our journey through astrology
Are our brothers found in Capricorn
Who like to live responsibly

When it comes to showing discipline
These Capris have it sorted
They can do just about anything
If they feel supported

The nature for things certain
Makes them dislike the mysterious
And wanting to be in control
Will often leave them serious

Not knowing what comes next
Is something they forbid
So when it comes to making plans
They can be pretty solid

If you want some independence
And someone who knows what's best
Then Capricorn's the one for you
Out of all the rest

It's important that we take the time
(especially at this stage)
To mention that the Earth, right now,
Is in the Aquarius Age

What that means is Planet Earth
Is going through a shift
Towards an Earth of kindness
And far from fear we drift

Slowly, slowly this age means
That we are breaking free
From all the things that hold us back
From living authentically

This is when the people rise
And break those shackled chains
It won't be long till love and trust
And unity remains

Now that's clear we can get back
To the star sign next, we see
Those born under Aquarius
Live quite progressively

They're independent, fun and strong
And love the human race
They'll fight for causes they hold true
And value active pace

The thing about being so free-willed
And so internally wise
Is that an Aquarius can dismiss
And refuse to compromise

If someone else does disagree
They'll wave them far away
They keep emotions deeply
And prefer not to relay

So if you want a fun ride
And someone who's unique
A person in Aquarius
Is someone you should seek

So now we've reached the end
I'd say we've come along with ease
The twelfth and final star sign
Are our giving friends in Pisces

Represented as two fish
To show the poles of their duality
A Pisces shows their kindness
By living life compassionately

The ones who are quite selfless
These fish are surely wise
You'll feel vulnerable and comforted
When looking in their eyes

The negatives about this
Means that they give too much trust
And then if this goes badly
Being closed off is a must

They like to play the victim
Meaning they can live quite sadly
But if their mood is up
These helpful signs can be quite friendly

If you're wanting some connection
To your inner intuition
A Pisces is the one to call
On your inquisition

Voilà! We've made it through the sky
We've passed each constellation
The stars are not just balls of gas
They're connected to creation

So please look up into the sky
On a clear and starry night
What is YOUR sun sign my friend?
Did I get it right?

SHINE

Once upon a Magic Time
Where time is no such thing
Exists a place where Love Is All –
The Source of Everything

But since there is no time in here
No night or even day
Once upon a Magic Place
Is more "correct" to say

And in this place where Love Is All
Resides a blessed sun
Whose necessary journey
Has only just begun

Now this sun in all its light
Is not just summer yellow
Oh no dear one, our friend The Sun
Is a multi-coloured fellow

This sun named SHINE holds every shade
Of every colour known
All the textures and the shapes
And every single tone

Shine's aura was surrounded
By the rainbow spectrum glow
The colours moved around him
In a universal flow

Red, orange, yellow, green,
Blue and purple too
But even more he had inside
Some colours that are new

Colours laced with sparkles
An ultra-violet hue,
Glow-in-the-dark and infrared
With neon colours too

Now I think it's time you know
That since Shine is a sun
Shine is both a "he" and "she"
Because she's everyone

And on one night... the 5th of May...
Or was it in November?
It doesn't matter I suppose
There is no time, remember?

So in a FLASH Shine looked around
And feeling so in love
Realised (quite suddenly)
There was no up above

There was no down below of him
No side. No left. No right.
The only thing that she could see
By being just so bright...

...was rays of him just shooting out
In all and no direction
And this is when Shine asked out loud
The Very First Question

"I am so bright. I shine as Love
I hold my own embrace
But what if I was not to be alone
In all this space?"

And as this thought echoed through
This vast infinity
There was now space between "here" and "there"
A sacred trinity

As Shine looked upon himself
A reflection in his heart
Knowing she was all of it
Still loved every part

Now that there were two of One
Shine knew this would be great!
"Hello there star. That's what we are
What shall we create?

I am you and you are me
We are all but one
We might seem separate, far apart
But we are both the Sun

We'll always be within ourselves
A fragment of the Source
And here's the best part of it all...
Intention with a force

We have the free-will choice to choose
Just what we wish to be
Knowing we are all of it
We are completely Free

Will you be a teacher?
Or someone who learns?
Will you know 'All of the Things'?
Or have some concerns?

Will you be a healer?
Someone people trust
Or someone who helps the world
When people are unjust?

Will you be a scientist
That people will call mad?
Or a freedom fighter
Combating the 'bad'?

Experience all that you must
To know yourself again
But know that feeling love so deep
May also bring you pain"

The other whole of the Sun
The mirror of the One
Began to feel fear inside
He spoke for everyone

"But what if I don't want to leave
This place so full of love?
What if I prefer to be the Whole
From up above?

What if I forget
That this place is my home?
What about the empty nights
That I will feel alone?"

"Forget you will," said Shine
So clear, so knowing and so wise
"But it is in remembering
That you begin to rise

You might forget, yes that is true
But in those times apart
Listen to your breath and body
Listen to your Heart

This is always You, my Star
Even down on Earth
You just get to play a part
Remembering your worth

I understand that being sad
Can make you feel alone
But without the 'bad' we feel
The 'good' cannot be known

It's nice to feel cared for
And hugged and rocked to sleep
It's beautiful to have a choice
Of memories to keep

It's cool to feel a chilly breeze
But only when it's hot
You can only be Who You Are
In knowing who you're not"

"Now I see," said the Whole
Of one half of the Sun
"So even though we seem like two
We are really one!

And even when I get caught up
In my 'created story'
I'll always be connected
To the Source and all its Glory

Wow this is fun! I need a name
A race and culture too
Height? Weight? Eye colour? Hmmmm...
Green, brown or blue?"

Shine smiled on beaming Light
That only Love could know
This was the beginning
Of a never-ending show

Shine knew well that Freedom-of-a-Choice
Was Key to Living
Shine knew how the Laws would work –
The getting and the giving

Shine understood the Truth of it
There was no risk involved
Shine knew at once that this would mean
Each story would be told

You see, it matters not to Source
What each person would so choose
All that is essential here
Is that no one could lose

So, my friends, I'm asking you...
What will you decide?
Imagine all the things you must
Let your heart run wild

Use your Creative Nature –
The thing you Really Are
And even though you're physical...
Remember... you're a STAR

Not someone who's famous
That's not the Star I mean
You Shine as Everything that Is
The Great Seen and Unseen

Be on your way you Precious Soul
Create yourself anew
In every moment, know that Shine
Is reflecting too

Be Brave. Be Bright. Be Love. Be Light
Be what you know is True
Be the You you want to be
Let the light SHINE through

Glossary for the awakened one

Aura: a colourful (yet invisible) light that surrounds the human body

Spectrum: all the colours in every shade from light to dark to light again

Universal flow: the energy that flows throughout the entire universe, the 'thing' that grows a flower, beats your heart and turns winter to summer

Ultra-violet: a purple-ish colour not seen by the human eye but which can be seen using special glasses/equipment

Hue: a shade or colour

Infrared: a red-ish colour not seen by the human eye but which can be seen using special glasses/equipment

Infinity: where time never ends and space is constantly expanding

Sacred trinity: the wonderful relationship between The Self and Other and the connection in between

Fragment: a part of the whole

Source: the Creator of Creation

Laws: universal laws, like the Law of Attraction and the Law of Cause and Effect

CHAKRAS

At one point in your life you've seen
A rainbow in the sky
There's just something about its glow
That'll always catch your eye

The way the colours blend as one
And how it makes you feel
Gives off a vibe that makes you think
That magic could be real

The colours aren't by accident
Although it seems this way
In fact, each colour has a point
And purpose to convey

We'll start with red because why not?
Let's take this one by one
Relax and settle into this
We've only just begun

The colour red does not exist
In rainbow light alone
'Cause when it comes to energy
You have your very own!

Every living being has
An energetic flow
A system called The Chakras
That emits a colour glow

We may not see these coloured gems
When looking at first sight
But when we know they're there at all
Then we can set things right

These swirling energies are filled
With wisdom we know not
Embedded in the truth of them
Is something we've forgot

And once we get connected
To these coloured energies
We'll realise that life is meant
To flow with constant ease

Now Sanskrit is a language
That has given these a name
So we can understand that
Every chakra's not the same

Starting from the bottom
Is a chakra at the base
It sits just by the tail bone
And is a sacred space

It's called the "Muladhara"
Or the Root in English terms
It helps the body ground to Earth
Connecting with the worms

It also helps us to feel safe
Survival is its game
It reminds us to feel worthy
And to move away from shame

Having stable thoughts
Like "I will always be provided"
Will open up this chakra base
And you will feel guided

Walking on grass barefoot
Will help you to connect
And feeling you're supported
Will have a grand effect

Earth is its elemental force
The root out of the four
Its power runs from inside us
Right to Earth's very core

Now as we move up body wise
We reach the orange phase
The Sacral chakra will assist
To feel in many ways

It knows about emotion
And how we can create
It drives our sexual urges
Moving us to find a mate

It's called the "Svadhishthana"
And it loves to move with flow
Being open with your loved ones
Will help this chakra glow

Its element is water
And it moves like out and in
So once you move with rhythm
Then your growing can begin

Now can you guess the next colour
That comes after this one?
I know you can. You're right to say
It's yellow like the sun

It's bright and bold and beautiful
Just like a gold sunflower
It helps us to take action
Through our very strong willpower

We have responsibilities
To listen to our soul
The Solar Plexus chakra
Helps us have some self-control

In Sanskrit it's called "Manipura"
Its element is fire
And when you have a strong belief
It takes your purpose higher

We need to have some discipline
To create identity
This helps us make a judgement
About who we wish to be

The next chakra that we will meet
Plays a colossal part
In linking all these energies
And it is called The Heart

"Anahata" is this chakra's name
Its colour is bright green
It has a huge magnetic field
Although this is unseen

Associated with true love
It helps us to go deep
In understanding others
Even those who are asleep

It shows us how to harmonise
Its element is air
The heart will always show us how
To show authentic care

The best way to connect with this
Begins, of course, with you
Kindness to the inner self
Is what the heart will do

You might not know this
But the heart gives off a loud vibration
An energy that has a strong
Relation to creation

It's always an important quest
To listen to the heart
Breathing deeply consciously
Is a perfect way to start

I promise when you do this
That your soul will surely float
Now let's connect with Chakra 5
Located in the throat

This chakra shines a crystal blue
And can be activated
When we decide to speak the truth
Which we deem underrated

But it is so imperative
To use words that portray
A way to express who we are
With what we wish to say

Our voice contains a sound unique
To each and everyone
And if the sound of 'Om' ॐ is used
Real progress can be done

"Vishuddha" is the Sanskrit name
Expression is the key
Connecting to your inner sound
Will set your shadows free

Its element is ether
And it can help express ideas
It wants us to speak confidently
By working with our fears

So always say just what you mean
And don't engage in lies
The next chakra to understand
Is in between our eyes

The centre of our forehead
Is where this gland is found
It helps us to see energies
That exist all around

It contains real psychic powers
That could help the human race
To understand perspective
When we're talking face to face

Our thoughts are telepathic
And contain a frequency
So thoughts that don't feel good to us
Affect us negatively

We'd benefit to train our minds
To always see potential
Because we know that to expand
Mistakes are an essential

This chakra shines with purple light
But some might call it violet
To activate this chakra
Would require peace and quiet

It helps for us to close our eyes
And focus deep inside
We often see intuitively
Which is our inner guide

And if you want to call it
By its O.G. Sanskrit name
It's pronounced as "Ajna"
Then the Third Eye it became

The element of Ajna
Is what we call pure light
And practising to meditate
Will give us true insight

So finally we've reached the top
We're on chakra number 7
Divinity flows down from here
Linking us to heaven

But not a heaven like a place
Existing far away
We access it right here and now
It's in us – dare I say!

The name is "Sahasrara"
And it emanates in pink
It wants to get you focussed
On what thoughts you often think

It's always bringing messages
From guidance up above
It shows us how to be apart
Of unconditioned love

This chakra is located
On the centre of our head
That's why it's also called the crown
Which is how it's often said

Connecting to this chakra
Will help you become aware
Of consciousness and wisdom
That you'll feel is always there

So now you know the chakras
You can make your body shine
When you actively make mind and soul
And Who You Are align

There are a lot more chakras
That most people haven't known
But my advice to you would be:
Explore them on your own

Once a chakra opens up
You'll start to feel the heat
The palms of hands have centre zones
And are also in the feet

The chakra we call "aura"
Is the hardest to describe
Responsible for giving off
A sense of someone's vibe

It encompasses our body
And our aura cannot lie
It picks up the vibrations
From the people we pass by

With all this information
You can lift your spirit higher
But you must make the effort
In yourself you must inquire

So when you see a rainbow
You'll know that you have one too
Now open up the gifts inside
You'll be grateful when you do

THE MAGICIAN AND THE FAIRY QUEEN

There is a land not far from here
Called Mooney Mushroom Town
The King has boots of navy blue
And on his head, a crown

His castle made of oak tree wood
Sweet-scented all the land
And every night under the moon
The King would sadly stand

Remembering a time so clear
When he was not alone
When Queen of Mooney Mushroom Town
Did share his gracious throne

She left the Earth and left the King
Alone in Paradise
And over time his loving heart
Had crystallized to ice

His skin began to turn a shade
Of lightly greyish blue
His happy-natured way of rule
Was gradually fading too

The mystics in this wondrous land
Started to fear the worst
No one had been sad or blue –
The King was now the first

The Mermaids in the ocean deep
Swam to the ocean floor
The Elves who lived in mushroom huts
Hid scared behind their door

Rock People and their faces wise
Began to disappear
And Sylphs, Nymphs, and Tree Spirits
Did quietly shed a tear

And even little Fairy Folk
Who usually saw the best
In every situation
Had no option – they confessed

The land became a barren place
The chirping birds had stopped
And even little naughty Imps
Their smiles suddenly dropped

The silence of the loneliness
Had filled the land until
It flowed onto the edge of town –
Reaching a house atop the hill

The aura of the King's upset
Had drifted through the door
It wandered up the flights of stairs
And reached the seventh floor

The only house atop the hill
(A miraculous creation)
Was home to Mooney Mushroom Town's
Marvellous Magician

Her hair so black it shone as blue
Her clothes of indigo
Her top hat made of silver silk
Her skin a golden glow

Although the magic of this town
Was evidently known
The Magician and her Black Rabbit
Preferred to work alone

She knew the land and all its folk
But never left the hill
She needed time to focus well
She needed to be still

She meditated with herself –
A really brilliant habit!
She wrote of Love in Magic Books
Connecting with her rabbit

But on this night, the sadness trail
Felt like a lonely song
The Magician frowned
She knew at once that something must be wrong

She packed her bag with magic things
She knew exactly what to bring
Her rabbit hopped along her side
She was off the see the King

***

Her journey was a lonely one
No magic folk around
But keeping to her Greater Work –
She followed signs she found

She journeyed through the forest path
Turning left and right
But suddenly, just out the woods
Something caught her sight

It darted round and through the trees
She caught sight of its wing
She heard it rustle in the leaves
And then she heard it sing...

A voice that made her stop dead still
A captivating sound
And then a presence moved on down
Floating to the ground

The Fairy Queen with long, green hair
And wings of shiny pink
Greeted the Magician
With a smile and then a wink

The Magician stood there quietly
A Fairy is no joke
She then flew to the magic girl
And finally she spoke

"Are you on a mission here?
A quest the same as mine?
We must head out right away
I've just received a sign

An Angel made of blueish white
Has come to give a warning
We must bring wonder to the King
Before tomorrow morning

The sadness in the King's own heart
Has gone so deeply black
That one more night of feeling it
Would mean he can't go back"

The Magician and the Fairy knew
How to move through time
They held their hands and closed their eyes
And chanted words that rhyme

The background of their lives
Became a blurry picture scene
They envisioned where the King would be
From where he's already been

They found themselves (the rabbit too)
Looking at the King
Who was looking at his love, the Queen's
Once engagement ring

The King looked up, his face so blue
Unbothered by the three
"Oh leave me be!" The King's head dropped
"Please just let me be..."

The Magician rambled through her bag
Of pens and spells and books
She pulled out one that shimmered gold
It's not all how it looks

"I know your pain our dear King –
The one we chose to lead –
But it would seem that on this day
Our service is in need

Feel yourself as loneliness
But then let Truth come in
You're more than this one role you chose
You're more than bones and skin

The Queen exists as all of you
In the moment here and now
She's with you every beat of heart
Don't question when or how

She's in her ring and in that chair
And things she loved to do
She's present when you think of her
She lives inside of you"

The King looked up with crying eyes
He sat up on the bed
A cloud of purple opened up
In the space above his head

The Magician and the Fairy gave
Each other one swift look
They knew the final key for him
Was something in the book

The Fairy ruffled through the book
That smelled of herbs and sage
She shuffled through with care and ease
Until she found the page

"It's time to know just who you are"
The Fairy sternly said
The world around had stopped in time
In its silence then, she read:

The Purpose Poem

"A grand endeavour that starts within
A goose-bump calling atop the skin
A pull to somewhere that feels like home
A script, a show, a book, a poem

Only love will bring true joy
You've tried in all the ways
But to surrender to yourself
Is the ending of your maze

The clarity will surely come
If you only trust
You must let go the ego mind
You must, you must, you must!

Your purpose has been realised
The path unfolds within
That guides the path before you
A light that's always been

From here it seems that knowing this
Was always what was so
So past and future have emerged
You stand amid the glow

A pinpoint in eternal now
Knowing what you know
Your heart exists eternally
Expansion must be so

So here you go... to nowhere
No place to really be
Except to be on Purpose now
You are forever free"

The King looked up. At once he knew
His arms had opened wide
The thing he'd searched for all along
Was always deep inside

He bowed and said "Thank you friends
For showing me myself
Excuse me now, I'd like to go
Have tea with Jed the elf"

The Magician and the Fairy turned
And took a silent bow
The rabbit hopped inside the bag
The quest completed now

The Magic had returned at once
The town was like before
Except the King now understands
Things just a little more

Glossary for the awakened one

Mystics: beings who have journeyed within themselves to find out who they truly are

Sylphs: an air fairy

Nymphs: a nature fairy

Meditation: contemplating in silence about the purpose of life/letting all thoughts go and being present with the breath and/or the heart

Chanted: saying powerful words of love in rhythm with the universal heart

Herbs and sage: plants used for healing

Ego mind: the mind that only thinks about thoughts and has no connection to the heart of the universe

Intuition flow: internal guidance, gut feelings about things

Eternal now: the Present Moment

THE LAW OF ATTRACTION

Have you ever seen the time
That showed the numbers 222?
Or had a funny feeling
That you knew was déjà vu?

Do you ever look behind you
'Cause you feel like someone's there
But when you turned around
All you could see was space and air?

Have you ever left your car keys
Where you leave them every day
But when you've gone to pick them up
They've travelled far away?

You know when you see something
Out the corner of your eye?
You know you've seen it in your heart
But nothing has passed by

I know you know that feeling
When you're thinking of a song
And then it plays right there and then
So you just sing along

Or even when you're feeling stressed
About a future date
But when it finally happens
It turns out better than great

These crazy, weird things all have
A simple explanation
They're just the way the universe
Is playing with creation

Some of these phenomena
Are quite hard to explain
'Cause no two people ever do
Experience things the same

See, we have the ability
To decide what we like best
And then we have the power
For these thoughts to manifest

We do this through subconscious
This is how it's often done
But when we're not aware of it
Then it is not-so-fun

In fact it's really scary
When we think we've seen a ghost
It's literally the very thing
That most people fear most

There's so much going on
Beneath the concept we call mind
Core beliefs and values
And learned fears of all kind

'Cause as we move quite naturally
Through the passages of time
We adopt some information
That we pick up in our prime

And often we are blind to these
And take them as our own
Unaware that thinking them
Will linger till we're grown

Some of them are helpful
Like the thoughts that bring us joy
But often they are harmful
And our spirit they destroy

You know now that your thinking
Has the will to manifest
So now you can try focus
Or at least just do your best

But this is then what happens
When the 'weird' things occur
So you can now experience
A life that you prefer

All that's really happening
Is that life will always match
The feelings you're projecting
Even bad ones – that's the catch!

So when you think of something
That comes true immediately
This is called in easy terms
A synchronicity

It's simply just what happens
When the universe aligns
With what you are intending
So it shows you clever signs

These signs have special meanings
This is so often the case
And if you try to ignore them
They might smack you in the face

They show up most in numbers
And the words we hear each day
There's no coincidence about
Whatever comes your way

It comes through an attraction
Which is a Universal Law
Its function is so accurate
It cannot make a flaw

It only knows togetherness
There is no separation
'Like attracts like' in this world
In every incarnation

Now how does all this help us
In a way that's beneficial?
Our only real option is
To see what's superficial

To focus on the things you fear
Is an energetic waste
It will reflect and manifest
Like a kind of copy-paste

But obviously I know that
Certain thoughts can be consuming
No matter how you try to forget
Some thoughts will leave you fuming

I promise, though, there is a way
A light, a grace, a hope
A way to flourish in this life
Not just to barely cope

The only way to let things go
And move on happily
Is honestly to smile it off
Don't take life seriously

The more you feel lighter
The more fun you will attract
Laughing at the journey
Is the only way to act

A thought that makes you grateful
Has vibrations very high
The kinder that your thoughts are
The less you'll have to try

The great Law of Attraction
Is something you can't ignore
So use it in your life
Now that you understand it more

Take the nasty comments
With a little pinch of salt
Loving those who judge you
Will make your fears melt

You're part of One Whole Universe
You cannot get away
Why would you even want to
When you came here just to play?

Only make a move
When you are sure it's joyous action
Remind yourself you have a friend
In The Law of Attraction

INTUITION

I've learned some things along my path
Some truths I wish to share
Information lost to us
But do you even care?

People say things all the time
About what they think is real
But I'm not here to make you think
I'm here to make you feel

At this time on planet Earth
With so much going on
Trusting what's inside of us
Is almost fully gone

We hear the news of this and that
The details are not clear
Because we've lost the way
To be *alive* right now and here

Depending on these 'others'
To show us how to be
Makes us disconnected
And anything but free

It seems that we've forgotten
That we have real worth
That we are meant to navigate
Our way around this Earth

With something that's inside us
Through guidance from The Source
Let's call this intuition
And let's say it's a force

An energetic signal
That sits inside our gut
That tells us who to stay with
Who to distance from and cut

You know just what I'm saying
You've felt this inner voice
And once you know just what it is
The whole world will rejoice

But if you choose to block them out
These very real senses
I'm sure you kind of know by now
There will be consequences

Not because you're bad inside
And need some sorting out
But because your purposed life
Should never be in doubt

You've come here with a mission
Agreed upon pre-hand
But this does not mean everything
In your life is planned

You have free will to choose the path
Of how you wish to be
But from perspective from the source
There's more to know and see

And that's what intuition is
It says when you're in sync
With what you've come to do this time
To have a conscious think

Not to follow blindly
What others seem to say
This is contradictory to
The natural, real way

Guidance is assured to us
It may be dim at first
But the more you feed it love
You'll satisfy that thirst

I know it's sometimes difficult
To trust that inner chime
But once you do, I promise you
You'll do it all the time

There is a way to move around
Where life is understood
The secret is in following
Whatever feels good

When you get sensations
That feel like butterflies
That's the way life helps you see
Not just with your eyes

Sometimes you'll be guided
To do things differently
To what your loved ones say you should
And best believe they'll be...

Angry, mad, outraged at least
Saying they know best
But trust me when I say
That in yourself you must invest

No one knows what's best for you
Except yourself of course
So trust that pull you feel inside
It's a magnetic force

Connected to the Universe
You are not something else
In fact you are this energy
You beat with life's heart pulse

So when you feel the goosebumps
Or an excited surge
That's when an inspiration for
The path will then emerge

And then is when you follow it
You trust and do what's right
No matter how it seems to all
No need to be polite!

Just seize the moment, do the thing
And watch what happens next
See how showing bravery
And courage then reflects

It's something that's inside us
Through guidance from The Source
Let's call this intuition
And let's say it's a force

THE SECRET KEEPER

Have you ever known something about someone else?
Something that widened your eyes?
Something that somebody heard from a bird?
Usually a shocking surprise?

Have you ever known something about someone else?
Something you knew wasn't true?
But when asked to repeat it to somebody else
You blurted the whole story through?

Remember when Pablo and Kyra and Troy
Went somewhere that one holiday?
Well boy do I have some gossip for you
You wouldn't believe the dismay!

Someone told Kyra who told it to Skye
Who told it to Avery Green
Who kept it a secret for a day and a half
But couldn't! And had to come clean

She told it to Raymond who couldn't believe
The craziness he had just heard!
He was told not to tell, but one couldn't hurt...
"I'll say that I heard from a bird"

He whispered to Cole but Cole did not like
To speak about others this way
He knew that a judgement about someone else
Could only cause stress and dismay

He frowned in distress and shook his head no
At the words floating into his ear
"No good can come from gossip like this, Ray
That's it! This secret stops here"

He walked straight to Troy who was a bit stunned
At the focus Cole had on his brow
"People are talking. Rumour's around
And I thought that you'd like to know now

We know you love Pablo. And Troy, that is great
You and I both know that's true
Don't let other people who are scared of themselves
Tell you how you should be you!"

Troy opened his mouth like he wanted to speak
And then closed it again 'cause he knew
That Cole had just broken the secret that had
Tormented his heart into two

"I've heard all the whispers and felt really bad
Because I knew it was talk about me
But thanks to an honest and wise boy like you
Our secret is finally free"

Now lucky for Pablo and Troy and their love
That someone like Cole was around
Not everyone's blessed with the knowledge to know
What to do when a secret is found

But wait, I'll stop here. This story you see
Is not about Pablo or Troy
The secret that's hidden beneath all this ink
Has to do with a charming young boy

Do you know that a secret, a real 'hush-hush'
Is something of magic indeed?
When someone keeps something locked inside their heart –
It summons a fiery need

A need to be heard, a need to be said
A need to shout out the truth
But fear will keep it inside one's own heart
Until gone are the memories of youth

But this is the thing. The thing that I know
Is a secret that's been hidden from you
The moment a secret is made in the heart
A keeper is awakened there too

***

The boy who has no name, they say, appears when he hears
A hidden truth that's locked away with keys controlled by fears
He moves around from world to world keeping all he's heard
Inside his key that's made of jade and shaped just like a bird

This boy, you've guessed, is what today and all this is about
It's time to tell you who he is... to let the secret out!

The Secret Keeper looks like light because he is not bound
To bodies, Earth and 3D touch and even taste and sound
His eyes are deep, a daunting void, dark circles underneath
He's always ever at a heart where secrets lie beneath

The moment someone hides the truth, a secret key is made
Which locks away the secret in a kind of masquerade
The secret then goes in a chest made of solid gold
And put inside the Keeper's cave where they can be controlled

The Keeper has a thousand chests, a million, billion more
He sees as people hide themselves and start an inner war
He's filled with darkness, sadness too – an endless stream of lies
His heart is filled with agony and this shows in his eyes

He's kept the burden of our lives since time first began
And will until the separate mind will cause the fall of man
For it will take a change of thought to set the Keeper free
To release him from our ignorance and throw away the key

Now it is not an easy task to face the core of pain
It takes the strong, the brave, the wise to break this bonding chain
That keeps a being like this boy bound to his own good heart
Who doesn't know that love and fear are polar worlds apart

The Secret Keeper has beliefs that say he's doing good
By being there for all the world (as if he ever could...)
But on one day, the world did change, never to be the same
When someone showed the Keeper that the secret's in his name

"Saying you're a 'Keeper' is your identity
This is how you see yourself and therefore it must be
But if you were to change your name to something more aligned
With who you'd really like to be – you'd serve all humankind"

You see, he thinks he's lessening the burdens of us all
By taking on and listening to every person's call
But as he hears, he takes the load of things that are not said
And now the secrets are not free, but trapped inside his head

They start to build a wall around his sacred energy
The Life Force that, if awakened, helps to set us free
No wonder that our Secret Keeper feels a hopeless dread
The flow is blocked – and now he feels a separateness instead

So when the Secret Keeper heard that he could change his fate
He knew that he should act at once before it was too late
He summoned all the keys he had and matched them with their pair
He closed his hands in gratefulness and said a little prayer

At once the keys unlocked the chests and secrets filled the room
The Keeper's heart had opened up just like a rose in bloom
He watched in awe the swirling mass of secrets in their storm
In one moment (in real time) the secrets did transform

They turned to light and burst in rays
He then fell to his knees
"I am now free," he realised
"I feel the love and ease"

The circles round his eyes had left his face as bright as day
Feeling this real joy inside took his breath away
And so for him, a life of truthfulness had just begun
He announced himself and said aloud: "I am The Honest One"

So what's the lesson here today? The one apparent thing?
To be the truest of yourself to all and everything
To stop the gossip where it stands and not spread lies around
Because in knowing truth is love, real hopefulness is found
And don't forget the story of The Keeper who became
His realest self by letting go of all the guilt and shame
Of any thoughts that people hide that they refuse to say
'Cause now he knows that he can speak the truth e-ver-y- day
The Honest One has now transformed just like a butterfly
The secrets are transparent now – so we can say goodbye

Glossary for the awakened one

Jade: a type of crystal that is green in colour and promotes harmony

3D touch: earthly, physical world

Void: nothingness, emptiness

Separate mind: also known as the ego mind, the mind that thinks you are unconnected to the universe and to others

Polar worlds: love and fear (opposites on the spectrum of emotion)

Sacred energy: universal energy of love flowing through each and every being

Life Force: universal energy of love flowing through each and every being

THE ELEMENTS

We're living in a universe
Designed in such a way
That each little component
Has an enormous part to play

The elements of nature
Assist in keeping us alive
Most people know that there are 4
When there are actually 5

Water, Fire, Earth and Air
It's most probable that you know it
The fifth one that's not so well known
Is what we call the 'Spirit'

They don't have a strict order
It's not like one is higher
Their value is all equal
So for fun let's start with Fire

But just before we light it up
It's important we discuss
That even though they're found outside
They're also inside of us

I'm well aware how odd it seems
But it's imperative I share
That you're also made up of these things
Water, Fire, Spirit, Earth and Air

The elements work through you
Inside you is where they are
So if you really want to feel them
You don't have to look too far

The Fire that's within us
Helps us to be passionate
It fuels our deep desires
And wants us to 'go for it'

It encourages our bravery
And provides us with the chance
To not just sadly move through life
But to get up and dance

There have been many symbols
That portray the Fire sign
And one's an upward triangle
With no dividing line

Associated with Fire
And connected to the sun
A Fire sign will not be still
It wants us to have fun

In terms of the 12 star signs
I'm sure you're curious
To know which ones have Fire
So one is Sagittarius

The 'go-getters' of the horoscope
Next is fiery Aries
But don't be fooled, they may be hot
But also sweet like berries

The last one of the Fire signs
We hear the Leo roar
So people with this star sign
Will have Fire in their core

For now, we will continue
To see how we can compare
The Fire sign we've learnt about
To the element of Air

The most valuable importance
Is the giving of our breath
'Cause obviously without it
Will result in instant death

The element that we call Air
Has a necessary link
To the nature of the thoughts
That we are so compelled to think

When using our imagination
Air wants us to reach high
An example of a star sign
That has Air is: Gemini

Our friends the light Aquarius
Are similarly Air signed
They're very intellectual
And Air makes them use their mind

The third and final star sign
That shares the element of Air
Is diplomatic Libra
Who likes things fair and square

An upward-facing triangle
Is the symbol of Air too
But unlike burning Fire
It has a line that runs right through

Moving onto Water
Which is the element of emotion
It makes you move with ebb and flow
Like the tide found in the ocean

Responsible for softening
Our habits for conclusions
It's linked to fairy-tales
And the mystery of illusions

Water breaks through structures
With a determining intent
Your body's made of Water too
About sixty percent

So hydrate to be healthy
And all the illnesses will drown
But unlike Air and Fire
Water's symbol's facing down

Now looking at the star signs
It's important that we know
The Water signs are Cancer
Pisces and Scorpio

These signs can be quite certain
In the way they choose to live
But Water makes them prone to be
A little sensitive

The element of Earth
Is so connected to the ground
That this is where our roots
To understand life can be found

Earth helps us be secure
And binds us to our home
It reminds us where we come from
So that we can freely roam

If we do the art of grounding
We will never be alone
We'll feel a sense of family
While living on our own

If we want to explore this element
The heart will help us enter
Earth's triangle is downwards too
With a line right through the centre

The three signs in the zodiac
Where Earth element is born
Is Taurus, Lady Virgo
And our stable Capricorn

These grounded, rooted beings
Will always keep things real
It takes a lot of effort
For their anger to reveal

The fifth and final element
Is the Spirit or the Soul
And this one is responsible
For making us feel whole

There is no doubt you have one
It's in every living thing
And when you become acquainted
You'll finally feel deserving

There really is no image
We can draw to symbolise
The Spirit that's inside us –
Except maybe the eyes

It's also not related
To just one sign in the sky
'Cause it exists in all of us
(Even sleepers qualify)

So next time you drink Water
Or light a Fire with some wood
You'll know these elements
Are linked to your livelihood

And next time you get muddy
Or take a conscious breath of Air
You'll know that the five elements
Are undeniably there

CPSIA information can be obtained
at www.ICGtesting.com
Printed in the USA
LVHW070059160622
721365LV00015B/485